TAXES FOR BEGINNERS

The Easy Guide To
Understanding Taxes
+ Tips & Tricks To Save Money

Table Of Content

Introduction

Welcome! First of all, thank you and congratulations for downloading this book "Taxes for Beginners". I really appreciate you putting your time and trust in me. I am truly convinced that this book is able to provide you with the value and information you are looking for.

If every year you have someone else doing your taxes without really understanding how you can minimize the amount of tax you pay and what influences the amount of income tax you pay, then chances are that you're missing out on a lot of additional money year after year. Taxes don't have to be complicated to understand. As long as you have a grasp on the basics then you can figure out ways to minimize the amount of money that you pay in taxes while maximizing the amount of money that stays in your bank account.

By the time you are finished reading this book, you'll understand how taxes are paid, what you can do to reduce the amount of taxes you pay, and have a basic understanding of taxes in general. With the techniques that you learn here you'll save money and time, by making your tax return audit proof and making sure that you aren't missing out on opportunities to significantly and legally reduce the amount you pay in taxes.

The tax laws in this country benefit small business and home-based business owners. You can enjoy doing what you love on the side and make a business from your passions while getting significant tax reductions and other benefits. The money that you spend on transportation, food, and lodging can reduce your taxes throughout the year and minimize the amount you pay each year.

Section I provides you with an overview of tax basics by going over how taxes started in the United States, how taxes are calculated, and how to uncover tax breaks that will save you money. Section II covers specific ways that you can reduce your taxes year after year by forming a business, teaches you about deductions, and explains the different ways to shelter your money.

Thanks again for downloading this book, I hope you enjoy it!

Section 1

In this section you'll understand what income tax is, what the government does with tax money that it receives, different ways to file your tax return, and the different tax forms that you can fill out at the end of the year.

Chapter 1 – Income Taxes In The United States

It is probably surprising to know that early American's didn't pay taxes. The Revolutionary War against the British was one that was fueled by taxation, so the early constitution prevented direct taxation for practical purposes. Instead of collecting tax from citizens, the government collected enough money to function with tariffs and duties on goods like liquor and tobacco products. In 1794 things changed when farmers revolted against tax collectors and Congress began to change how taxes are collected.

Later on as American's waged war with other nations, taxes were levied in order to pay the expensive cost to go to war with another country, or to fight a civil war. The American Civil War brought about a basic income tax that closely resembles our current tax system and at that time the Internal Revenue Service was founded, which handles tax payments for American citizens and noncitizens.

In 1913 the 16th Amendment was added to the Constitution to form an income tax since before then direct taxes had to be levied in proportion to a state's population that was having a negative effect on world trade and standards of living for poor citizens. Within a few years, more of the United States population was paying income tax with the tax rates increasing and the exemption levels decreasing with time.

Tax rates increase often, and decrease depending on who is president. With social programs and healthcare to pay for, there won't be too many significant reductions to the amount of taxes that people pay for a while. Programs, services, and wars have to be paid for and the US taxpayers are the ones that pay the bills.

Chapter 2 – What The Government Does With Income Taxes

The government collects money from taxpayers in the forms of corporate and individual income taxes, estate taxes, gift taxes, social insurance taxes, and excise taxes. The government spends the money it collects from taxpayers three ways, as mandatory spending, discretionary spending, and to pay off federal debt. There are many different categories of programs and services that taxes go toward, all of which benefit American's in some way.

Mandatory spending goes toward Social Security, Medicare and healthcare, unemployment, agriculture, veterans' benefits and transportation. These programs make up mandatory spending because they are considered permanent. These programs do not have set dollar amounts and instead the amount of money that is allocated to each program depends on the amount of people who are eligible for each service.

Discretionary spending is money allocated to more than a dozen different services and each budget is determined by congress every year. A portion goes to the military; some goes to housing, education, food, science, energy, environment, and many other areas that the government subsidizes. Spending on these areas isn't seen as mandatory so Congress can shift the money it allocates to different areas based on need.

In total, most of the taxes you pay go toward Social Security, Medicare, and the military. The other categories make up anywhere from one to four percent of the budget, which is very minor compared to the amount allocated to the top three categories.

Chapter 3 – Income Tax Law

Income tax in the United States is known as a progressive tax, because as your taxable income increases, the amount of tax that you pay also increases. Depending on your annual income, you'll fit into one of many different "tax brackets."

Individual Taxpayers Tax Brackets 2015

If Taxable Income Is Between...	The Tax Due Is...
$0 - $9,225	10%
$9,226 - $37,450	$922.50 + 15% of the amount over $9225
$37,451 - $90,750	$5156.25 + 25% of the amount over $37,450
$90,751 - $189,300	$18481.25 + 28% of the amount over $90,750
$189,301 - $411,500	$46,075.25 + 33% of the amount over $189,300
$411,501 - $413,200	$119,401.25 + 35% of the amount over $411,500
$413,201+	$119996.25 + 39.6% of the

	amount over $413,200

If you make $50,000 a year then you fall into the 25% tax bracket, however you won't end up paying 25% of your taxable income, but rather 25% on the amount that you earn over $37,450. Since the tax is progressive, you'll pay $7,038.75 on an income of $50,000 ($5156.25 + $1,882.50 [15% of $12,550]) instead of $12,500.

The tax bracket that you qualify for depends on your tax status. The different options are Single, Married Filing Jointly, Married Filing Separately, Head of Household, and Qualifying Widow with Dependent Child. Your status is determined by your family situation on December 31st of the year you're filing taxes for. If you fit in two different categories at that time then you can decide how you'd like to file your taxes.

Single taxpayers are those who are not married. Check out the above tax brackets if you'll be filing a single return to determine how much you'll pay in taxes.

Married Filing Jointly is for couples that are married and filing a single tax return together. You'll have a combined income, deductions, exemptions, and credits that determine your taxable income.

Married Filing Jointly Taxpayers Tax Brackets for 2015

If Taxable Income Is Between...	The Tax Due Is..

$0 - $9,225	10%
$9,226 - $37,450	$922.50 + 15% of the amount over $9225
$37,451 - $90,750	$5,156.25 + 25% of the amount over $37,450
$90,751 - $189,300	$18,481.25 + 28% of the amount over $90,750
$189,301 - $411,500	$46,075.25 + 33% of the amount over $189,300
$411,501 - $413,200	$119,401.25 + 35% of the amount over $411,500
$413,201+	$119,996.25 + 39.6% of the amount over $413,200

People who are married also have the option to file separately. There are usually more benefits that come with filing together, but it's an option for people that make a close income to their spouse and end up being placed in a lower tax bracket separately, if a couple is close to getting a divorce and don't want to deal with post-divorce complications, or for couples that don't want to be liable for their spouses tax bill.

Married Filing Separately Taxpayers Tax Brackets for 2015

If Taxable Income Is Between...	The Tax Due Is...
$0 - $9,225	10%
$9,226 - $37,450	$922.50 + 15% of the amount over $9,225
$37,451 - $75,600	$5,156.25 + 25% of the amount over $37,450
$75,601 - $115,225	$14,693.75 + 28% of the amount over $75,600
$115,226 - $205,750	$25,788.75 + 33% of the amount over $115,225
$205,751 - $232,425	$55,622 + 35% of the amount over $205,750
$232,426+	$64,998.25 + 39.6% of the amount over $232,425

Heads of Household are people who are single or unmarried and support a qualifying person. A qualifying person is a child or relative in your care. Heads of Household are placed in lower tax brackets and have a higher standard deduction from standard individual taxpayers. This is a great way to file if you are a single parent and looking to save money on your taxes.

Head of Household Taxpayers Tax Brackets for 2015

If Taxable Income Is Between...	The Tax Due Is...
$0 - $13,150	10%
$13,151 - $50,200	$1,315.50 + 15% of the amount over $13,150
$50,201 - $129,600	$6,872.50 + 25% of the amount over $50,200
$129,601 - $209,850	$26,772.50 + 28% of the amount over $129,600
$209,851 - $411,500	$49,192.50 + 33% of the amount over $209,850
$411,501 - $439,000	$115,737 + 35% of the amount over $411,500
$439,000+	$125,362 + 39.6% of the amount over $439,000

A widow or widower who has lost their spouse can file their taxes as married filing jointly the year the spouse dies, and as a qualifying widow/widower for the two year period afterward, unless he or she remarries during that period. This filing status helps to get over the financial sting that occurs when losing a spouse.

Qualifying Widow with Dependent Child Taxpayers Tax Brackets for 2015

If Taxable Income Is Between...	The Tax Due Is...
$0 - $9,225	10%
$9,226 - $37,450	$922.50 + 15% of the amount over $9225
$37,451 - $90,750	$5,156.25 + 25% of the amount over $37,450
$90,751 - $189,300	$18,481.25 + 28% of the amount over $90,750
$189,301 - $411,500	$46,075.25 + 33% of the amount over $189,300
$411,501 - $413,200	$119,401.25 + 35% of the amount over $411,500
$413,201+	$119,996.25 + 39.6% of the amount over $413,200

Chapter 4 – The Different Tax Forms

There are many different ways to do your taxes and it's up to you to decide if you'd like to do them yourself, or if you'd like a professional to handle filing your taxes for you. When it comes time to file your tax return, it's important that you are organized. Throughout the year, keep good financial records and have your W-2s, interest statements, school taxes, property taxes, receipts and other information on hand for when you need it. Also have a copy of your previous years tax return, as you can deduct the amount of income that you paid in taxes the next year. A little organization goes a long way, filing taxes doesn't have to be a complicated process if you are correctly prepared.

First you should learn if you need to file at all. If you are a United States citizen or a resident of Puerto Rico then it's likely that you have to file. It depends on your gross income, filing status, and your age as to whether or not you need to submit a return, or whether someone else can claim you as a dependent or include your information on their tax return without you having to do it yourself. Check out the Department of the Treasury Exemptions, Standard Deduction, and Filing Information to determine whether you have made enough income based on your situation to have to file taxes.

There are three main filing forms that you can use to file your taxes. Depending on your situation you'll fill out either a Form 1040EZ, Form 1040A, or Form 1040. If you do not qualify for a 1040EZ or a 1040A then you have to fill out Form 1040, and it might be best for you to use Form 1040 anyway so that you can itemize deductions and receive more of a tax break than you would with the other two tax forms.

Form 1040EZ is a simple tax form but you have to meet certain requirements in order to be eligible to complete your taxes with this form. You also cannot claim itemized deductions and risk possibly overpaying your taxes. In order to be eligible to submit a Form 1040EZ you should file as a single individual or as a married couple filing jointly. You and your spouse must be under the age of 65 as of the last day of the tax year and not blind. You also cannot claim any dependents, must have a taxable income of less than $100,000, only have income from wages, salaries, tips, unemployment compensation, scholarships, grants, or up to $1,500 in taxable interest. You also cannot claim any adjustment income, cannot claim any credits other than the earned income credit, and cannot be a debtor in a chapter 11-bankruptcy case.

If you don't meet all of the requirements above, then you can fill out Form 1040A, which lets you report other types of income and payments from your IRA, account. You also cannot claim itemized deductions with a Form 1040A, so you are limited to certain adjustments to your income and your income must be less than $100,000. If you don't meet these requirements then you should fill out Form 1040, where all income, deductions, and credits can be reported.

There are different forms that you can file with your taxes if you file Form 1040A or Form 1040. These are known as "schedules." Schedule A allows you to itemize your deductions and it's the form that you have to fill out if you are claiming anything other than the standard deduction. An example of the deductions that you can list on this form includes medical and dental expenses, certain forms of taxes, interest payments, and work expenses.

Schedule B is used with both Form 1040A and Form 1040 and allows you to list various forms of income, interest, and dividend payments that you've earned during that tax year. You are only required to complete Schedule B when you earn over $1,500 of taxable interest or ordinary dividends, you've received interest from a seller-financed mortgage and the buyer resides at the property, or if you have accrued interest from a bond.

Schedule C or C-EZ is used with Form 1040 if you report self-employment income. With this form you can calculate your business net profit or loss that influences the amount of tax that you pay and is added to your income on Form 1040. Schedule C-EZ is a simplified version of Schedule C that you qualify for if your business meets simple accounting requirements by the IRS.

Schedule D is for capital gains that occur when you sell a capital asset during the year. Usually this form is used with the selling of stalks, but it can include selling other property such as a home or car. The assets that you sold are taxed differently depending on whether it's a short-term asset that you've had for less than a year, or a long-term asset that you've owned for over a year.

Schedule EIC is for reporting an earned income tax credit. You can qualify for this if you meet the correct specifications. If you have qualifying children and your income falls below a certain level then you can claim this refundable tax credit. Schedule EIC can be used with both Forms 1040 and 1040A.

The final form that you attach to your taxes is Schedule SE for non-withheld Social Security taxes. When you're self-employed then you have to pay social security taxes on the amount of income you make since you don't have an employer collecting that money for you. With Schedule SE you will figure out how much money you need to pay for self-employment tax.

Chapter 5 – Ways To File Taxes

One option that you have for paying your taxes is with an IRS-approved tax preparation service that you complete online or on your computer. These are often sold in retail stores or office supply stores and is a convenient way to complete your taxes with a computer application. There are different versions for personal tax filing, business tax filing, or both. Some software applications that you might be familiar with include H&R Block and TurboTax. This is a great way to file your taxes if you have a simple tax return where you don't claim lots of deductions or have too high of an income.

Some applications that you can use on your personal computer to complete your tax return can be submitted online and therefore require Internet access. There is also tax preparation software where you can print off your taxes and mail them to the IRS that don't require an Internet connection, but it takes longer to file your return and receive a tax refund if you qualify for one.

Software is nice because it walks you step-by-step through the process of inputting your income, deductions, and state tax information, and will double check that all of the information you've input is accurate. It's very easy to mistype something, so you have to be careful with your inputting and notice if you make any mistakes while doing your taxes so that you don't underestimate what you owe or overpay because of a simple error.

Your taxes can be submitted manually or electronically depending on what you prefer. Sending your tax information by mail takes a bit longer and requires that you send a check to a separate location, so it can be much simpler filing electronically instead. You can also give the IRS your bank information to pay your taxes electronically or to automatically deposit your tax refund after a few days of processing.

Tax day is April 15th, so you want to have your tax return sent to the IRS at that time or a little bit before. If for some reason you cannot complete your taxes before that day then you should file for an extension either electronically or by mail. With an extension you'll receive 6 additional months to file your taxes, which allows you to get all of your paperwork in order. Filing an extension by mail can be completed with Form 4868.

It's important that even when you apply for an extension, that you make some form of payment toward your taxes if you believe that you owe money. You can request additional time to pay your taxes by calling the IRS if you feel that you can come up with the money in 120 days. Otherwise you should fill out Form 9465 or Form 9465-FS, which lets you set up installment payments on your taxes and makes it easier to pay throughout the year.

If you don't like to use tax preparation software on the computer, you can always complete your taxes manually. The IRS prefers that you submit your taxes by electronically filing because it reduces the chance that there are mistakes, but tax forms can be found at your local library or post office if you would like to complete it by hand. The taxpayer package should include instructions and all of the forms that you need to complete your taxes whether you're filing a 1040, 1040A, or 1040EZ.

Use a black pen while completing your taxes and input your income and any deductions that you qualify for. Make sure that everything is complete, accurate, and that you have signed and dated the tax return before mailing it. If you are worried that you haven't done everything correctly, it's a good idea to have someone else look over your calculations and reduces the chances that you'll be audited.

Mail the IRS your tax return as well as any of the additional forms that you've filled out with your taxes. Place your social security number at the bottom of each page so that in case any of your papers get separated, that your identification number is listed. You'll have a state tax return as well as a federal tax return which should go to different places, make sure to remember to put your return address on the envelope.

Once you have mailed your tax forms, then you should also make a payment if you owe money. You can have an electronic funds withdrawal remove any money that you owe from your account, which is the simplest and quickest way to pay your taxes. You can also pay with a credit or debit card, by mailing a check, by sending a money order, or by enrolling in the Electronic Federal Tax Payment System.

The same rules apply for filing an extension with a paper form if you need it. Just fill out Form 4868 before the deadline. Just remember that you shouldn't do this to delay the payment if you don't have enough money for your taxes. Instead, give the IRS a call and let them know how soon you can come up with the money to pay your taxes and complete Form 9465 if you need to pay in installments and it will take you over 120 days.

The other option that you have for completing your tax return is to have a tax professional do it for you. It's a good decision to talk to a few people who can prepare your tax return for you before hand, as they might also know significant ways to save you money later on in the year. Some people turn to certified public accountants, attorneys, or tax preparation offices to complete their tax returns, so you can start your search for the right person there.

Give all of your information to your tax professional before the filing deadline and make sure that they have your contact information in case they have any questions about the documents that you've given them. Set up a time with them when you can go over your tax return and review that everything is completed correctly. During this meeting you'll sign and date each return if everything looks good.

If you use a tax professional, make sure that you give yourself and them enough time to properly review all of your documents, and to file your taxes. If you have a complicated return, it's best to leave it in the hands of a professional who is used to completing all of the tax forms, and that knows how to set up a business to receive the maximum deduction for your taxes.

Chapter 6 – Exemptions, Deductions, and Credits

So now you understand the process of filing your taxes, but lets dive deeper into explaining what everything is so that you understand what information you'll input on your tax return. This section will explain tax exemptions, tax deductions, and tax credits.

There are many different tax exemptions that you can claim on your taxes. Exemptions help you reduce or eliminate the amount of taxes that you pay entirely. Exemptions are similar to deductions, and most taxpayers qualify for certain exemptions to reduce the amount of taxes that they have to pay. Certain organizations are also exempt from paying income tax such as charities and religious organizations that benefit the public that it serves.

People who are not claimed as a dependent on another person's tax return can file personal tax exemptions. This is a fixed amount that is applied toward the amount of money that you owe in taxes. If you are single then you qualify for one exemption on your return. If you are married then both you and your spouse qualify for two exemptions.

There are also dependent exemptions that you can claim if you have other people that you provide financial support for. Children under the age of 19 or the age of 24 if they're students can give you a break on your taxes. Relatives that live with you can also qualify as dependents as well as your parents that you support financially.

If you own a business that doesn't operate for profit and meets all of IRS' requirements, then you can apply for a tax-exemption. If your business provides valuable services to the public then you can reduce the amount of money that you have to pay in federal income taxes, but you have to keep good financial records if the business wants to keep its tax-exemption status. You can also receive a break from your taxes by donating money to these charities and organizations.

Your business may also be able to receive tax exemptions if you qualify for specific state, county, and municipal government programs. These programs support businesses that stimulate the global economy and saves money for your business. Check with your tax professional to find out what kinds of programs exist in your area and your surrounding areas.

Tax deductions are similar to exemptions, where they reduce the amount of money that you have to pay on your taxes. This works because a tax deduction lowers the amount of taxable income that you have and therefore lowers your tax liability. There are two types of tax deductions that you should be aware of while completing your taxes. The first is the standard deduction, and the second is the itemized deduction.

The standard deduction is a set dollar amount set by the IRS that you could take each year. The standard deduction works for most people because you don't have to calculate anything, you don't have to hold on to receipts of expenses, and there aren't any additional tax forms to fill out. Here are the standard deductions for the 2015 tax year:

Filing Status	Standard Deduction Amount...
Single	$6,300
Married Filing Jointly	$12,600
Married Filing Separately	$6,300
Head of Household	$9,250
Surviving Spouse	$12,600

Itemized deductions on the other hand do have to be calculated and you must keep track of all your financial information, but it could end up saving you additional money by lowering the amount of taxable income that you have. If you own a home, contribute to a retirement plan, or make contributions to charity then chances are that you can receive even more of a reduction than the standard deduction amounts listed above. In order to claim deductions you should use Form 1040A or Form 1040 to file your taxes.

The categories that you can deduct from your taxable income include health care costs, income taxes or state taxes, property taxes, mortgage interest, personal property taxes, interest on certain investments, contributions to charity, losses due to theft or casualty, job-related expenses, tax preparation fees, home office expenses, and gambling losses.

If you are going to itemize your deductions, it's important that you keep track of all your expenses and payments for the amounts that you are claiming in the event that the IRS audits you. There are also limits to how much you can reduce your taxes using itemized deductions depending on how much income you make and thresholds that you have to surpass in some categories in order to reduce the amount of money that you pay in taxes, which you might not meet in every case. It's good to talk to your tax professional about whether it would benefit you more to itemize your deductions, or whether you should take the standard deduction.

Tax credits are different from tax deductions, but similarly reduce the amount of tax that you have to pay. Whereas tax deductions reduce the amount of taxable income that one has to pay, tax credits reduce a person's tax liability directly. Some tax credits are also refundable which means that if your tax liability falls below $0 that you can get a tax refund with the credits that you apply.

Chapter 7 – How Your Refund Is Calculated

How you calculate your taxes is fairly simple and has to do with how much money was withheld from your paychecks versus the amount of money that you should pay in taxes based on your tax bracket's total tax payment. If you withhold more money than what is due at the end of the year then you get a tax refund. If you withhold less money than what is due at the end of the year then you have to pay taxes to the government.

Every time that you receive a paycheck, the amount of money that you get paid ends up being less than you owe because money gets "withheld." This is to make sure that people don't spend all of their income without having enough money saved to pay taxes at the end of the year. Withholding is just a way to ensure that you pay taxes on every portion of your income that you receive so that you don't have too large of a sum to pay once tax season comes.

It might seem that your employer is deducting a lot more money than required of your tax bracket, but that's because income tax, Social Security tax, Medicare tax, and state income tax are also being deducted from your paycheck. You can decide the amount that you want to be withheld from your paycheck when you fill out your W-2 at the end of the year and contribute more to your tax payments so that you don't have lots of money to pay at the end of the year.

Taxable income is more than just what you make at your job. Of course wages, salaries, bonuses, commissions, and tips are included in your taxable income. There are also some forms of income that most people don't think about earning that you should include in the amount of income that you receive for the year.

Taxable income includes fees that you receive for acting as an estate administrator, trustee, or executor, the fees that you receive from jury duty, and the fees you collect while serving on a board of directors. Awards, contest winnings, and prizes are also taxable income. Cancelled debts, severance pay, unemployment benefits, freelance income, interest and dividend payments, royalties and lottery winnings also stand as taxable income and should be reported on your tax return.

Federal taxes aren't the only taxes that you have to pay for receiving income. Most states and the District of Columbia have individual state income taxes that you have to pay. States apply different rules than the federal government does on income, so where you live has an impact on the amount of state income tax you'll pay at the end of the year.

Section 2

Now that you have a grasp on how you file taxes and what income is considered taxable income, let's discuss different ways to reduce your tax liability so that you can build wealth.

Chapter 8 - Owning Your Own Home-Based Business

There are two main income tax laws. One allows deductions for employee items like IRAs and 401ks while the other assists small and home-based business people by allowing them to make tax deductions on their house, their employees, transportation, dining and more. Building a home-based business allows you to save money every year on taxes by reducing the amount you pay each year to the legal minimum.

The things that you do on a day-to-day can end up saving you more money than you would earn working a second job. Many of the expenses that you have can be deducted on your taxes legally after you start a home-based business. After starting a home-based business you'll also be able to set up a pension plan and travel around the world as long as you conduct a certain amount of business.

Even if your business isn't profitable, the government will subsidize your business by giving you a return on your income taxes for up to two years afterward or you can carry over the loss into future income tax returns for up to 20 years. It's risk free and there's potential that your business is successful and gives you an even greater return from what you do every day.

You can start any type of home-based business that you'd like based on what you like to do or something that you're good at doing. You can sell products or engage in services out of your home, or you can consider a network marketing position if you enjoy getting out of the house. If you already have a small business or a home-based business, as long as you do the right activities then you can take advantage of this great opportunity for American small business owners.

Chapter 9 - Deducting Your Entertainment Expenses

You can deduct your expenses by following a set of rules while doing the things that you love to do. Most entertainment expense deductions are limited to 50 percent, but there are exceptions to that rule. For example if you went to dinner with a business prospect and there is a business reason for the meal or entertainment that you are participating in, then you can deduct it from your taxes as a business expense. There must be a business purpose for the meal or entertainment, it has to take place in a place where you can conduct business, and if you conduct business before, during, or after then you can legally deduct the meal.

The important part about being able to deducting your entertainment or meal is to audit-proof these activities. You can do this by keeping all of your receipts for business meals and entertainment, especially those that are over $75. Write down who was at your business meeting, their occupations, official titles, and any other information needed to show a business relationship. Also include the time, date, and location of where the entertainment took place, write down a specific reason why the business meeting took place, and list how much it cost (being sure to keep your receipt if it's over $75.) If you keep these records in a timely fashion then you'll cover yourself if the IRS ever audits you.

Now lets say that you want to entertain a business client outside of a business setting. In this case, you're allowed to deduct 50 percent of your entertainment expense if it's "associated entertainment." Associated entertainment takes place in a non-business setting where there is no business discussion. As long as you have a business discussion on the same day preceding or following the associated entertainment, then you can deduct this cost from your taxes. Again, be sure to keep track of your who you met with, where it occurred, why it occurred, and the amounts of money that you spent to audit-proof your return.

If you would like your significant other to join you during an entertainment event, you can as long as the person you are discussing business with also brings their significant other along as well. You can't deduct a meal with just yourself and your spouse or significant other because the IRS knows that you are closely connected, but as long as you tie it into the business meeting and your business associate brings someone else along then you can deduct the expense.

To track your cost of personal meals you can list down how much you normally spend on food and expense the excess cost of your food over your average meal price. This also works the same way if you split the cost of a business meal with your business partner, which is known as a Dutch-treat deduction.

There are a few exceptions where you can deduct the full cost of your expenses instead of just 50%. If you are engaging in an activity that is a business promotion then you can deduct the whole cost of your expenses. Home entertainment can also be deducted, sometimes more so than going out to eat at a restaurant. As long as you conduct business with the people you are entertaining, as long as it doesn't seem like a personal event, then you can deduct the cost of your food and beverages 100%.

Chapter 10 - Deducting Your Vacation Costs

While you're on a business trip you can deduct 100 percent of the on-the-road expenses such as the cost of lodging, laundry, and dry cleaning. You can deduct half of your food expense while traveling as well. The only thing that you need to need to do is stay somewhere other than your home or a place that you go often. As long as you spend the night in a place that you rarely go, then the trip is considered business travel.

You can also deduct the costs of your spouse or significant other by employing them to your business. He or she has to have a reason for accompanying you on the trip, and if your partner can earn you income while on the trip or has licensing in the business then you can deduct their expenses as well.

If your business trip takes you to a foreign destination, you can also claim that the weekends are business days if you conduct business on the Friday and Monday of the trip. Even if you aren't working, your expenses are tax deductible. This also works on Federal holidays, allowing you to vacation and save money on taxes every year. Even the days that you travel to your destination are considered business days as long as you take a direct route and don't have too many non-business diversions.

When you take your business vehicle to go on a trip then you're still able to deduct the cost of travelling. Up to 300 miles per day can be deducted from your taxes, so split up travel days to make use of this. All of the lodging and meal expenses can be deducted, except for the cost of taking additional people, so if you were to spend $50 for a single room and it costs $75 to get a double room, you can deduct the $50 and the leftover $25 is a nondeductible expense.

Cruises can also be tax deductible if you attend the right ones. If you attend a cruise that is hosting a convention related to your business and more than half of the time you're on the cruise you are spending time on business then you can get a deduction of up to $2,000 a year. The cruise has to be registered as a U.S. vessel and the port has to be in the U.S., but as long as you take log of the business activity you do each day and the amount of hours you spent in business seminars. Conventions and seminars are also tax deductible if you spend at least half of your normal working hours conducting business activities, even if it doesn't happen to be on a cruise.

Chapter 11 - Making Sure That You Are Audit-Proof

In order to gain the maximum amount of deductions for your home-based business, you have to keep good documentation of your activities. Expenses under $75 usually don't have to be proven with receipts except for when it comes to lodging receipts. It's important that you keep good records of where you went and what you did, and keep receipts from your on-the-road travel separate from your transportation expenses.

Keep a log, diary, or tax organizer to list down all of your expenses on the day that it happens in order to prove to the IRS what money you spent. When you go to conventions and seminars, you should explain the amount of days you spent there and prove that you had more business days then personal days. When you travel outside of the U.S. more than two thirds of the days that you travel should be business days. If you can maintain good records then these expenses are 100% tax deductible. In order to prove that a trip is for business, you can also document business intent for the trip by listing correspondence sent to business partners, emails, and phone calls.

Keeping good information is also important when it comes to transportation expenses. As a home-based business owner you are able to deduct the mileage when you drive for business use. Depending on the percentage of time that you use your vehicle for personal and business use determines how deductible your business automobile is. If you don't keep good records about your driving, then your transportation costs won't be tax deductible.

In order to keep good records, you should list the total miles, the total business miles, the total commuting miles, and other personal miles whenever you drive. The records should show that you are using your vehicle for business use and although you don't need to write down all the travelling you do daily and you can get away with listing your miles at the end of the week, it's easiest to just write down the information whenever you get in your car to drive home.

There are a few options that you have when it comes to logging your miles for the IRS. You can create a one-day log where you list all the times you use your car, the nature of your trip, and determine the amounts of mileage for each stop. This is quite a bit of information, so you can create a 90-day log if that's too tedious. You basically follow the same process for 90 days to substantiate how you use your vehicle the rest of the year if you follow similar driving patterns for the whole year.

The third option that you have is to log your miles is to use the first-week rule. During this time you keep an automobile log for the first week of each month and show that your business use was similar during the rest of the month. You still list out your appointments, but you only have to calculate the mileage that you use for the first week of every month. The fourth option is to list out only your personal use for 90 days, and compare the odometer to find the percentage of time that you spend using your vehicle for business and for personal reasons. This option is a lot easier for most people, and it's easy to figure out how many miles you use your car for business transportation with some simple math.

Conclusion

Understanding taxes doesn't have to be complicated. If you want to build wealth and secure the financial future of your family, it's important that you understand how tax laws work, and how to pay as little as legally possible toward taxes. With the simple tricks that you have learned about the benefits of starting a home-based business, you'll be able to save lots of money on the things that you already to and at the places that you already go. It also gives you the opportunity to travel, speak to people, and share what you love to do with the world.

The most important thing is that you take action and start your home-based business. Prepare yourself for the changes that you have to make in order to meet the IRS requirements. Start taking good notes about your daily activities, learn how to log your mileage, and start saving receipts whenever you go out to eat with business partners. It might seem like a hassle at first, but the significant saving that you receive from building a home-based business will pay off for years to come.

Now that you know some of the significant tax savings that you receive from starting a home-based business, now it's time to do it! You'll earn more income with a home-based business than you could with a second job, and you'll have the opportunity to travel around the world, meet new people, and sell your products and services to others. You can work primarily from home if you enjoy spending time alone, or you can use it as an opportunity to network with new people and live an exciting life. The tax laws benefit those who are self-employed and understand the many different tax benefits that are available for business owners.

Thank you again for downloading this book!

I hope it was able to help you to understand taxes.

The next step is to implement what you have learnt.

Finally, if you enjoyed this book, would you be kind enough to leave a review for this book on Amazon?

Thank you and good luck!

www.ingramcontent.com/pod-product-compliance
Lightning Source LLC
Chambersburg PA
CBHW070416190526
45169CB00003B/1289